Black's Picture Sports
GOLF

Black's Picture Sports
GOLF

Charles Price · Sports Illustrated
Revised by Peter Ryde

Adam and Charles Black · London

This edition first published 1976 by A & C Black Ltd
35 Bedford Row, London WC1R 4JH

ISBN 0 7136 1611 3

Cover and photographs on pages 8–9, 16, 28, 31, 32, 37, 40, 43, 54, 73, 79, 83, 84, 90, 94 Sporting Pictures (UK) Ltd; 12–13, 21, 88–89 Bert Neale

Authorised British edition
© 1976 A & C Black Ltd
Originally published by J B Lippincott Company in the United States of America as *Sports Illustrated Golf* by Charles Price and the Editors of Sports Illustrated © 1970, 1972 Time Inc

Set and printed in Great Britain by
Page Bros (Norwich) Ltd, Norwich

Contents

1   The Game and the Course

THE GAME

Anyone taking up golf has to realise at the outset that it is an appallingly difficult game to play well. The technique of hitting a golf ball, mastery of which is still no guarantee of playing good golf, involves almost every part of the body – feet, legs, hips, shoulders, arms, hands, even the head – all coordinated to a fine art.

Ben Hogan, after twenty-five years of playing golf, several of them as the game's leading money winner, took his swing apart and put it back together in somewhat different form. To everyone's astonishment this turned out to be an improvement. Tony Jacklin, a good enough golfer to be leading the field after three rounds of the 1970 US Open championship, had to be reminded by his friend Tom Weiskopf not to swing too fast in the final round. The American stuck the one word 'tempo' inside Tony's locker, and the trick worked. Michael Bonallack, one of the greatest amateur golfers in the last thirty years, was not content with having won three British championships and a host of other events as well. He decided that, faced with increasing competition from young players, he must step up his own game. To do this he went to work on his swing, and reduced the ducking movement in it which had caused him, at one time, to be described as swinging like a coal-heaver.

While the act of hitting the ball is intricate enough, it is nevertheless only a part of the complexity of the game. Luck enters into it to a degree which some consider

Muirfield: home of The Honourable Company of Edinburgh Golfers

8

distressing. Golfers often hit a shot exactly as they intended only to see the ball bury itself in a bunker, while a badly mis-hit ball might scuttle its way as if by magic into the hole. Everyone has had the experience of playing badly yet winning a match, and on another day playing well only to lose. In a professional career that covered nearly forty years, the great Walter Hagen managed to record only one hole-in-one, yet there are many who score regularly in the nineties but still have half-a-dozen aces to their credit. How can that be explained in logical terms?

In order to keep the innumerable situations that arise all over the world within a manageable framework, the Royal and Ancient Golf Club, in collaboration with the United States Golf Association, has compiled forty-one rules of play and thirty-four definitions of terms relating to the game, as well as an appendix covering everything from the proper dimensions for flagsticks to the legal markings on iron clubs. These are published in a booklet that hardly anybody bothers to read and which almost nobody thoroughly understands.

To the casual golfer, who seldom plays any course other than his own, the rules seem unnecessarily extensive. Yet despite the fact that no two courses are alike and that a single course seldom plays the same two days running, they do cover virtually all the incredible number of situations that can arise in a game that is played in nearly as many countries as there are United Nations. Thus, a rule that had its origins on a course by the sea in Scotland centuries ago will cover adequately a situation that might arise tomorrow on a newly constructed course in a Continental resort. It will do so because in each case the same basic principle is involved: play the ball as it lies and the course as you find it.

ORIGINS

The word 'golf' is derived from the Germanic word 'kolbe' meaning club. Apart from its name, golf is entirely Scottish in origin, despite some arguments to the contrary.

One of these arguments is that the game began in Holland, a supposition supported by the existence of numerous old masters depicting the Dutch playing a game which bears some similarity to golf, but a good deal more similarity to a crude form of hockey.

What we do know for certain is that golf was played in Scotland five and a half centuries ago, and we have no record of it being played then anywhere else. Whatever type of game may have been played elsewhere, it was the Scots who first combined the features of hitting a ball cross-country, with a variety of implements, to a hole in the ground, without interference from an opponent. Moreover it was in Scotland that golf was kept alive in the seventeenth and eighteenth centuries when it was beginning to lose its popularity elsewhere. In the early days golf was played on seaside links which had the status of public parks and were overrun with sheep, cows, and countless rabbits. For protection against the biting wind that blew in off the sea, these animals scraped out hollows in the ground and the holes they left filled with sand from the adjoining beaches. In this way originated the sand bunkers which now form such indispensable hazards. The links were not used for golf and grazing alone; open to the public, they were apt to become the scene of horse racing, cricket matches or cattle shows. At any time they might also be taken over by soldiers drilling, washerwomen bleaching their linen, fishermen spreading out their nets, housewives beating carpets, nurses sunning babies, or children at play.

In 1744 golf began to be ruled informally by a group known as the Honourable Company of Edinburgh Golfers who first used the nearby links of Leith, later moving to Musselburgh, and ending up at Muirfield, some 25 miles east of Edinburgh. Ten years later, a similar group, the Society of St Andrews Golfers, came into being with its own set of rules. Slowly this club, across the Firth of Forth from Edinburgh, began to take over the leadership of the game. The royal title was bestowed on it in 1834 by King William IV and the club

The Old Course at St Andrews

12

became known as the Royal and Ancient Golf Club of St Andrews. Its influence continued to spread, and the rules that it spelled out in 1754 formed the basis of those in use today. St Andrews also set the fashion in courses of 18 holes which endures to this day. In the early days St Andrews had twelve holes. In a round, however, ten of those holes were played in duplicate. You started by playing eleven holes in a row, then turned and played ten of the same holes backwards, finishing the round by playing a solitary one near the place from which you had begun. Thus a complete round at St Andrews consisted of 22 holes. In 1764 the Society knocked out two of their holes. Since these holes were played out and back in the course of a round this was reduced from 22 to 18 holes, a number that came slowly to be accepted as standard. But there were plenty of exceptions. For a time Leith had only five, then seven, while at Prestwick in the 1860s the Open championship was decided over three rounds of 12 holes. But today a round consists of 18 holes, properly played in their correct sequence.

THE COURSE

The hole The expression 'hole' has two meanings in golf. Firstly it is the receptacle, $4\frac{1}{4}$ inches in diameter, which is sunk into the putting surface to a depth of at least 4 inches. Into it is stuck a flagstick, nearly always adorned by a flag which sometimes bears the name or number of the hole. One of the most distinguished exceptions is Merion, a famous championship course outside Philadelphia in America, which has wicker baskets attached to the flagsticks. Secondly it is the entire area from the teeing-ground, through the green, to the putting surface.

The teeing-ground The teeing-ground is the starting place from which play on the hole is begun, usually an area where the turf has been specially levelled and prepared. That part of it from which the ball may legitimately be struck is a rectangle, two clublengths in

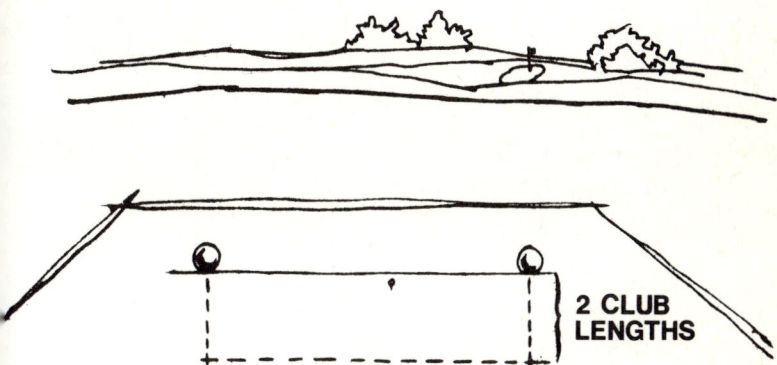

TEE

Figure 1. The teeing ground—or 'tee'

depth, the front and the sides of which are defined by two markers. For the first shot the ball is usually placed upon a tee, a wooden or plastic peg about 1 or $1\frac{1}{2}$ inches long. The word 'tee' is also used as an abbreviation for teeing-gound ('Which is the way to the tenth tee?'). The context in which the word is used makes the sense clear. The ball when teed may not be placed in front of or outside the line of the two markers, but it may be placed up to two club-lengths behind their line. Once the ball has been struck from this position it is said to be in play, but a ball knocked accidentally off the tee in addressing it is not in play and may be replaced.

Markers There are usually three sets of markers on each hole at varying distances from the putting surface.

15

Gary Player – playing out of a shallow bunker

16

The farthest back (usually yellow, though in America more often blue) stretch the course to the utmost and are reserved for championship occasions; the total difference in length between these and the most forward markers for women (usually blue or green) can be as much as 600 yards. In between come the normal markers for men, which are usually red in this country but white in the United States.

Order of play In a match the order of who is to play first off the tee is determined by the 'honour'. The first player at the opening hole (in a competition according to the order of names on the drawsheet) continues to play first off succeeding tees, or continues to hold the honour, until the person or persons with whom he is playing completes the hole in fewer strokes, whereupon his opponent takes over the honour and strikes first off the tee. From the tee the ball is played towards the hole 'through the green'. Strictly speaking, this expression means the whole area of the course except for the tee for that hole, all hazards, and the putting surface into which the hole is set. (Each of these exceptions has its own special rules.) However the area is further divided into two sections: fairway and rough.

Fairway and rough The fairway is the best way to the hole, a broad swathe mown short but not as closely cut or well prepared as the green itself. Anywhere outside this is rough, which can vary greatly in character. In the United States, for example, it may be no more than grass an inch or two higher than the level of the fairway grass; but it may also include bushes, scrub, trees, stones, rocks, or bare ground which greatly add to the player's difficulties. In Britain it is generally much tougher, with heather, gorse, thick woods and long grass prevalent in different parts of the country. In an attempt to get more people round in a shorter space of time, newer courses are generally being built now with lighter rough.

17

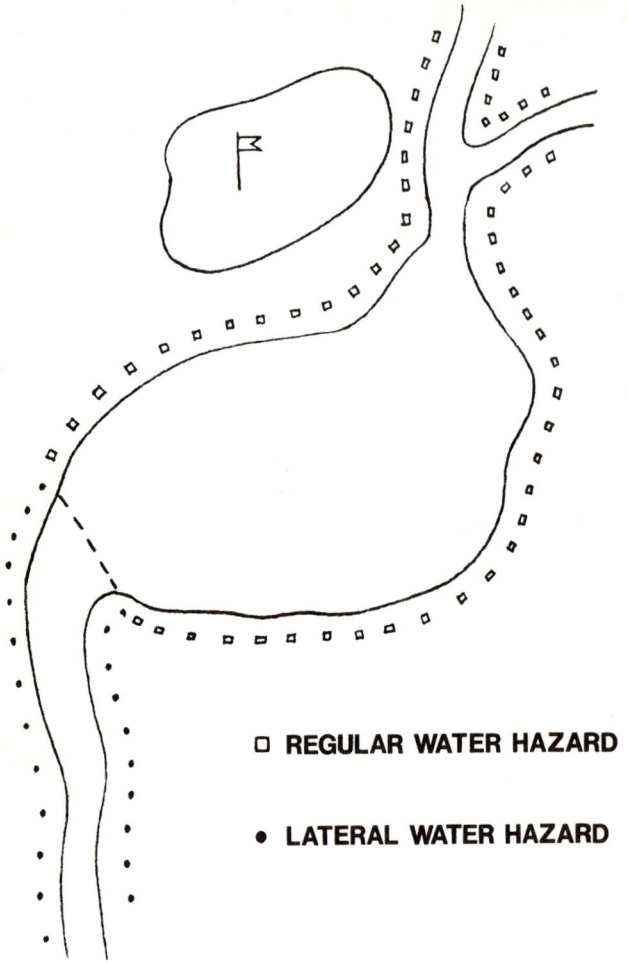

Figure 2. Water hazards

18

Hazards   Hazards may lie within the area either of rough or fairway. One type of hazard is the bunker, an area of ground, often a depression, usually covered with sand. In shape and size bunkers vary greatly. They may be no more than 'pot' bunkers, described once by Bernard Darwin as being 'just large enough to hold one angry man and his niblick', whereas some seem to stretch for hundreds of yards. Bunkers in Britain are usually deeper than those in America, and are often faced by steeper banks.

Another form of obstacle is the 'water hazard' which is defined as any sea, lake, pond, river, ditch or any other natural channel though which water runs, even though that channel might be temporarily drained of water. A ball hit into it may be played where it lies, though the player risks getting nothing more than a good splashing. If it is picked up it must be dropped somewhere behind the point of entry under penalty of one stroke. An elaboration of this is the 'lateral water hazard' which is a water hazard, or part of one, running nearly parallel to the line of play and so situated that it is not possible to drop the ball behind it while keeping the point of entry between the player and the hole. The penalty here is again one stroke and the area in which it may be dropped is within two clublength's but not nearer the hole – in other words it may be dropped either side of the water.

An important rule common to all three hazards is that you may not 'ground' your club before making the stroke, this is so that you may not test the texture of the sand or the depth of the water in advance.

The green   The ultimate target in every case is, of course, the hole, or cup as it is sometimes known in America. But all except the very best players would regard the green or putting surface as their primary target. Striking the ball into the hole from off the green involves some degree of skill but an even greater degree of luck. Therefore it follows that the first objective should be the surface from which one is most likely to play the ball into

19

the hole even though a particular point in the rough may be nearer. A ball which finishes on the putting surface but 30 feet from the hole represents a sounder shot than one which finishes off the green. Once at a crucial hole in a tight match for the British Amateur championship, the great Bobby Jones purposely hit a long second shot to the green 60 feet off the line of the flagstick in order to avoid a tiny bunker that was directly in his way to the hole and not 20 feet from it. Jones knew from his vast experience that any shot on or near the putting surface, no matter how far from the hole, would be easier to play than one from that bunker. Although Jones did not win the hole, neither did he lose. Two holes later he finished the match and went on not only to win that championship but to achieve a feat unique in the history of the game, the winning of the British and US Opens and the Amateur championships of both these countries in the space of one year. In later years he still considered his decision to avoid that bunker at all costs one of the more intelligent he ever had to make in the fulfilment of that unforgettable golfing season.

The putting surface – or green – is all the ground specially prepared for putting. Since the putt involves rolling the ball along the ground instead of lofting it through the air, it is important that the surface should be true, especially in tournaments involving large sums of money. The putter, the shortest club in the bag, has no loft and may be of almost any shape, although in an attempt to make easier this most difficult aspect of the game many clubs have been invented which have been ruled illegal by the authorities. Greens may be immense – at St Andrews where there are double greens it is possible for a putt to be as much as 60 yards long – but harder obstacles still for the putter may be the mystifying contours of some greens, and the lightening speed of others; many a golfer faced with a downhill putt over a closely mown surface has struck his ball right off the green.

Par Every hole on a golf course falls into one of three

Sunningdale: the fourth green on the New Course

categories: par-three, par-four or par-five. With allowance being made for two strokes on each of the greens, par for a course is the total number of shots that an expert golfer would be expected to make on the eighteen holes. It implies playing without error and without any accidental strokes of luck. Theoretically, the expert golfer is expected on a par-three to reach the putting green in a single stroke from the tee and to take two putts. On a par-four he is expected to reach the green in two, and on a par-five in three, strokes. The basic rule for deciding on par for a hole is its length, although the severity of its hazards may have some bearing on it. A hole is measured from the middle of its teeing area through mid-fairway to a point halfway between the front edge of the putting green and its back edge. A par-three is any hole up to and including 250 yards in length, a par-four from 251–475 yards, and a par-five anything over 475 yards. (For women these yardages run anything from 40 to 70 yards less.) The total of all the individual pars adds up to the par for the course. Most modern courses have a par of 72, consisting of ten par-fours, four par-threes and four par-fives. But this is by no means a universal rule; a number of courses have a par of 70 or 71, and pars as low as 69 and as high as 73 or above are not uncommon.

Par implies golf without error or luck, yet you can achieve par figures in any number of different ways. The nature of the game is not *how* but *how many*. Thus it is possible to make a par by missing the green in the right number of shots but by taking only one putt – or even no putts at all. Although par implies faultless play, it may often be improved upon. You may play a hole in one stroke less than par – in professional golf the standard is so high that this happens frequently – in which case you are said to have scored a 'birdie'. You may even play a hole in two strokes fewer than par. At a par-three hole this would mean a hole-in-one (or 'ace' as the Americans call it), perhaps the ultimate thrill in golf. On a par-four or par-five a score of two strokes fewer than par is called an 'eagle'. Golf even has a term for the hole that is done in

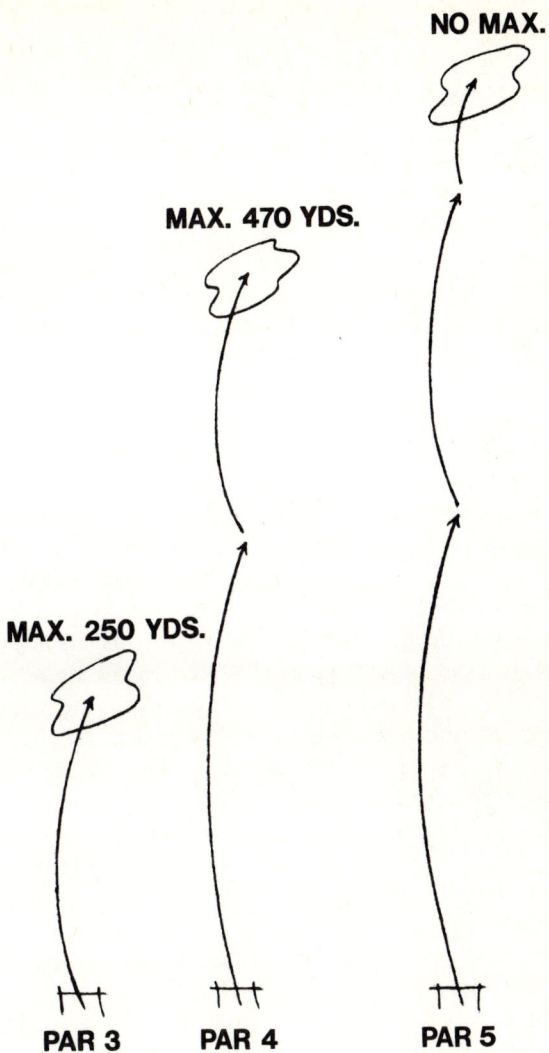

NO MAX.

MAX. 470 YDS.

MAX. 250 YDS.

PAR 3   PAR 4   PAR 5

Figure 3. Par for a hole

three strokes better than par. In Britain this is called an 'albatross', whereas the Americans call it a 'double-eagle'. This is a rare occurrence and is more likely to take place at a par-five, where a long second shot might hit the green and roll into the hole, than at a par-four, when the tee shot itself would have to be holed.

Far more probable and common is the 'bogey' – originally an American term for a hole played in one more than par, but one that is rapidly passing into common English usage. A 'double-bogey' is of course taking two strokes more than par at a hole. Higher scores than this have no name, perhaps because they are regarded as unspeakable and, when made, unprintable.

Match play and stroke play There are two basic forms of the game: match play and stroke play. Each form has its own rules. Match play was the original form but nowadays the British Amateur Championship is one of the very few major championships played in this way. Stroke play is specially favoured by the professionals who rightly think that it gives a fairer reflection of merit and does not involve them in the humiliation of a personal defeat. In stroke play the competitor who holes the course in the fewest number of strokes over a given number of rounds is the winner. In match play the winner is he who wins the greater number of holes. A hole is won by the player or side who holes in the fewest strokes. If the number of strokes taken by each side is the same the hole is said to have been 'halved'. The match is won when a player is leading by a number of holes won which is greater than the number of holes remaining to be played. Normally matches are played between one, or two players on each side. One player against another is officially called a single. A threesome is a match in which one plays against two, each side playing one ball, the team of two playing alternate shots. A 'three-ball' is a match in which three players compete against each other, each playing his own ball. A foursome is a match with two players on each side each playing alternate shots at one ball. Outside the

British Isles this form of the game is almost extinct and although the professional match between Great Britain and the USA, the Ryder Cup, includes a series of 'foursomes , it is largely kept alive by a strong minority in Britain who consider it to be the finest way of playing. A 'four-ball' is a match in which two players play their better ball or better score against that of two other players. A 'best-ball' is a match in which one plays against the better ball of two or three opponents. The 'four-ball' is probably the most popular format at the moment and is often combined with a method of scoring known as a 'Nassau'. This consists of three matches rolled into one. One point is allotted for the first nine holes, another point for the second nine, and another for the whole eighteen. Thus if you were to lose the first nine one down and win the second nine one up, the eighteen-hole match would have been halved.

Handicap   The great equaliser in golf competition is the handicapping system. Roughly speaking, your handicap is the number of strokes over par in which your average game is played. Let us assume your average score is 90 over a course whose par is 72. Your handicap would therefore be eighteen. Thus in a stroke-play competition, eighteen strokes would be deducted from your score. In match-play the situation is more complicated, the longer handicapped player receiving a proportion of the difference between his handicap and that of his opponent. Should your handicap (or in match-play, the difference between your handicap and your opponent's) be less than 18 – say 10 – you would receive strokes at the holes indicated on the score-card. The order in which handicap strokes are distributed depends roughly on the severity of the hole, the first stroke being awarded at what is considered the most difficult hole.

Etiquette   Etiquette is – or should be – strictly observed in golf. Golf is more enjoyable when these unwritten rules are observed. One of the oldest games ever devised by man is also one of the most civilized largely because of its strict code of politeness and consideration. Below are listed some of the procedures laid down by the Royal and Ancient Golf Club – follow them closely:

1   No one should move, talk, or stand close to or directly behind the ball or the hole when a player is addressing the ball or making a stroke.
2   The player who has the honour should be allowed to play before his opponent or fellow-competitor tees his ball.
3   No player should play until the players in front are out of range.
4   In the interest of all, players should play without delay.
5   Players searching for a ball should allow other players coming up to pass them; they should signal to the other players to pass, and should not continue their play until those players have passed and are out of range.
6   Before leaving a bunker a player should carefully fill up and smooth over any holes he has made.
7   Through the green, a player should ensure that any turf cut or displaced by him is replaced at once and pressed down, and, after the players have holed out, that any damage to the putting green made by the ball or the player is carefully repaired.
8   Players should ensure that, when putting down bags or the flagstick, no damage is done to the putting green, and that neither they nor their caddies damage the hole by standing close to it, handling the flagstick or removing the ball from the hole. The flagstick should be properly replaced in the hole before the players leave the putting green.
9   When the play of a hole has been completed, players should immediately leave the putting green.

Priority on the course   In the absence of special rules, singles, threesomes or foursomes should have precedence of, and be entitled to pass, any other kind of match. A single player has no standing and should give way to a match of any kind. Any match playing a whole round is entitled to pass a match playing a shorter round. If a match fails to keep its place on the course and falls more than one clear hole behind the players in front, it should allow the match following to pass.

Peter Oosterhuis — chipping from off the green

2 The Clubs

The clubs used in golf are divided into two categories: woods and irons. The primary purpose of woods is to gain distance; the primary púrpose of irons is to produce accuracy. But the longest wood player in the world is not a good one unless he can use woods with a certain degree of accuracy. And the straightest iron player in the world is not a good one unless he can hit irons with authority; that is to say, unless he can draw from each the forward thrust that has been built into it by the clubmaker. You can hit an iron to the green as straight as an arrow, but the shot will be all but worthless if the ball drops 15 yards short of the flagstick. By the same token, a 300-yard drive is wasted if it lands in rough or a hazard. Accuracy, then, is an integral part of wood play and distance is an integral part of iron play.

WOODS

In the early days of golf, the first four woods were referred to, in order of length, as the driver, the brassie, the spoon, and the cleek. Today, they are simply called the one, two, three and four woods, although most golfers still refer to their one wood as a driver. In the past decade, the five-wood has also come into favour. While most golfers think it is an innovation, it is in fact a club that years ago was referred to as a baffy. It is a valuable club for a beginner to concentrate on. Women seem to be particularly adept with it, which is not to imply that there is anything feminine about it. There are many tournament professionals who swear by its effectiveness.

The one wood   The one wood – or driver – is commonly used off the tee on those holes where distance is a major factor: par-fours and par-fives. For most men, the driver is expected to propel the ball somewhat in excess of 200 yards; for ladies, perhaps 30 yards less. Since the shaft on the driver is the longest of any club – usually 43 inches – and since the loft on its face is the shallowest, it is geometrically the most difficult club in the bag to play with accuracy. However, it is used to hit the ball to that area of the golf course which permits the widest margin for error – the fairway. Sometimes, when the lie is particularly favourable, the driver can also be used off the fairway, but this takes great skill. Of the few British professionals who attempt this shot with any degree of regularity, Christy O'Connor is perhaps the best exponent.

The two wood   The two wood is slightly shorter than the driver, and has more loft which gives it rather greater accuracy. It was originally designed to provide the utmost distance off the fairway, when the ball must be played off turf rather than a tee. Nonetheless it is a club that requires considerable experience to use effectively from the fairway, and as a result it has within recent years fallen into disfavour among club golfers. Among professionals, Neil Coles is particularly adept with it. You might play ten rounds of golf and not find ten opportunities to use it, and so, many people leave it out of their bag.

The three wood   The part that the brassie used to take is today mainly taken up by the three wood, one of the most utilitarian clubs in the bag. Most middle handicap golfers can hit the three wood in the neighbourhood of 200 yards – ladies, proportionately less – and they use the

Tom Weiskopf – playing a long iron shot

Ireland's John O'Leary

club with a degree of accuracy they often cannot expect from their long irons. They use it to approach the greens on long par-fours and for positioning the ball on second shots to par-fives. One of the truly great three wood players in the history of golf is Jack Nicklaus, who often uses his off the tee when he considers accuracy to be more important than length. He loses some valuable distance but gains invaluable accuracy. Nicklaus, the strongest player in the game, knows that golf is basically a game of strategy, not muscle.

The four wood   The four wood is a spoon with additional loft. It substitutes for the three wood when the ball is not lying on the fairway quite as cleanly as you would like, or when the ball is lying in light rough and distance is still a factor. On occasions, you can extract from it practically the same distance as you can from a three wood, although probably without any greater degree of accuracy. It is an extremely versatile club. It supplies the power of the three wood with almost as much loft as a middle iron. Dai Rees has been one of the best exponents of the club in Britain – even in his fifties he was still achieving great accuracy with it.

The five wood   The five wood has a shorter shaft than the four wood and as much more loft than the four wood as the four wood has over the three; but it can supply the utmost distance you can get from your longest iron while also giving out the loft you can extract from a shorter club; say, your five iron. Among average players there are innumerable shots which can be played with a five wood. In the top flight of golfers, Lee Trevino uses this club most frequently.

In summing up, then, it may be said that your soundest combination of woods – taking into consideration the fourteen club limit – is a driver, a three wood, a four wood and a five wood. The two wood is a specialty club, whereas the four wood can replace the three wood on occasion. So stick to the one, three, four and five.

IRONS

The basic list of irons stretches to nine. Historically, they were called the driving iron, mid iron, mid mashie, mashie iron, mashie, mashie niblick, spade mashie, spade mashie niblick, and niblick. (This nomenclature varied widely among clubmakers, however.) Today, you can ignore the names, none of which has been used in years by golfers. Some purists still refer to their nine iron, with which they make most of their short approaches, as a niblick. But its role has largely been supplanted by a ten iron and eleven iron, which incongrously, still go by names: the pitching wedge and its father, the sand wedge, from which it derives so many characteristics. Strictly speaking, they are utility clubs but so useful that hardly anybody attempts to play golf without them any more. Their stroke-saving effectiveness in contemporary golf is beyond exaggeration.

The one iron   The one iron, or 'driving iron', is a club that nobody but an expert should attempt to use and hardly anybody but a touring professional actually can use. It has almost no loft and a shaft almost as long as a five wood. With it, the ball must be struck with precision timing beyond the means even of a scratch-player – and he would have to be playing golf almost daily to be sharp enough to bring it off with consistency. There are professionals who would not dream of carrying one in their bags. Its purpose is to hit the ball the same distance as a three wood with a very low trajectory; for instance, in order to keep the ball low in a high wind that might very well blow a three wood askew. Jack Nicklaus, as might be expected, is perhaps the leading exponent of it today. Peter Oosterhuis among British players makes specially good use of it, and his reputation for scoring birdies is largely based on his accuracy with it. Since there are so few golfers who are vain enough to think they can play in this image, manufacturers do not even bother to make the club other than by special order. In short, now that you know what it is, forget it.

The two iron   Because it, too, has a long shaft and very little loft, the two iron remains the roughest club in the bag for the average player – which explains why so many of them leave it out. Also, the five wood gets the same job done. Generally speaking, the two iron hits as far as the four wood but with a lower trajectory; which explains why it is often preferred in a wind.

The three iron   A matched set of irons today traditionally begins with the three iron as it is the first of the so-called long irons that the average player can use with any sense of security. He needs the three iron because its range, for him, is approximately 170 yards, the distance from which he can first begin reasonably to expect to hit a green and stay on it. Taking another situation into consideration, most par-threes are within the range of a three iron. So he has his confidence in it to back him up. It may be that the best advice for using a three iron (or any other long iron) is to swing it as though it were a short iron. That is to say, handle it in the same tempo. You cannot possibly add any more length to it than the manufacturer has built into it.

The four iron   The four iron is the link between the long irons and the mid irons. Its precise use is difficult to describe to a beginner. Suffice it to say, there will be any number of occasions when the three iron will be too much club for the shot at hand and the five iron not enough. Golf is a game of strategy, but it is a highly instinctive one, too. After some experience you will know when a shot calls for a four iron instead of a three or five.

The five iron   The five iron is the cornerstone among a set of irons. Its range lies at about 150 yards – the average distance you will need to reach a par-four hole, with your second shot, or most par-three holes on the average golf course. Its usefulness extends even beyond that, for it is the club you will most want to use when chipping from off the surface of the green. Furthermore, since it falls midway in the spectrum of the irons, it calls upon the swing of which the swings on all other clubs are variations. You cannot do better than to practise it alone if your practice time is limited. Swing a two iron with the same speed as you swing a five iron or a nine iron and you cannot go too far wrong mechanically. It may be a compromise, but you will get results. The name of this game is how many, not how.

The six iron As the four iron is the link between the long irons and the mid irons, the six iron is the link between the mid irons and the short irons. Its range lies in the neighbourhood of 140 yards. Since so many factors other than distance have a bearing on your selection of clubs – the direction of the wind, the position of bunkers around the green, the elevation of the putting surface – again your knowledge of when to use a six iron rather than a seven or a five iron will come largely from instinct, something that can be developed only through experience. Even then you will never be utterly sure. In fact, proper club selection is a problem no one ever thoroughly masters. Indeed, it seems to become more and more complex as your experience increases. As Bobby Jones once said, 'Golf is the only game I know that becomes more difficult the longer you play it'.

The seven iron The seven iron is the first of the so-called short irons. Strategically, the short irons are used when accuracy is almost your entire purpose; which is to say, when reaching the green is no longer a problem. Your immediate concern is hitting the green and placing the ball as close to the flagstick as possible. Short irons must be hit smartly, to be sure, but they are used with something less than a full swing. You are playing what is known in golf parlance as an 'approach'. Consequently, there is no sense in hitting a full nine iron when you have an eight iron in your bag, nor any sense in playing a full eight iron when you have a seven.

Tony Jacklin

The eight and nine irons   If the range of your seven iron is about 130 yards, the range of your eight iron can be expected to be 120 yards. (Roughly, there should be 10 yards' difference between each iron.) Any distance below 110 yards then, becomes the territory of your nine iron, the ubiquitous 'niblick', which many golfers use for any shots down to 40 yards and even for chips when little run on the ball is desired.

The pitching wedge   From about 80 yards down, however, most golfers rely heavily on the all-purpose 'pitching wedge'. It supplies the most loft among the irons and, when struck properly, the most backspin, thereby stopping the ball in the shortest space, which is important when the flagstick is placed close to a hazard. The closer you get to a green, the more your pitching wedge will be called upon. While it must be played with authority, as any club should, it is nevertheless used on what might be looked upon as half shots or even quarter shots, the most delicate shots in the game. There is probably no finer exponent of wedge play in Britain than its most recent Open champion, Tony Jacklin.

The sand wedge   The 'sand wedge', a club developed not quite forty years ago, has revolutionised scoring golf. In the hands of a professional, it is, like the pitching wedge, a deadly effective weapon. Until the development of the pitching wedge, in the late forties, it was even used off turf, and still is by some pros on odd occasions. You, however, would be wise to confine its use to sand bunkers. Get confidence in the sand shot, and you have gone a long way towards playing like an experienced golfer.

The putter   This is a straight-faced club – one with no, or very little, loft – which is used to roll the ball along the ground and into the hole.

A full complement of clubs, then – to summarise – might be the one, three, four and five woods; the three through nine irons; a pitching wedge, sand wedge, and finally, of course, a putter, giving you a bag of fourteen clubs, the maximum number allowed. All sorts of variations on this list are possible. An American bandleader, Fred Waring, who has been a devotee of golf for half a century, uses no irons whatsoever, except his sand wedge, which is the one indispensable iron in the bag. Waring uses twelve woods, all substitutes for every iron up to and including the pitching wedge. While such a bag of clubs is not advisable, particularly for a beginner, it shows that much improvisation is possible within the scope of the game.

Judy Rankin, one of the top USA women golfers, showing a firm grip

3   The Grip and the Swing

THE SWING

The golf swing is initiated by the combination of three physical attitudes. The first, and easily the most important, is the grip, or the placement of the hands on the club. The second is the stance, or the position of the feet on the ground. The third is the address, or the posture of the body in relation to the direction in which you want the ball to travel.

Once set in motion, the golf swing is composed of a series of synchronised, controlled movements and conditions: straight left arm, cocked shin, steady head, square clubface, bent left knee, tucked right elbow, sliding hips, shoulders under, firm left side, follow-through and so on through a list that seems to grow lengthier and more confusing the longer you play the game. Most of them can be mastered, and consequently forgotten, by the use of the same natural action you would apply to any physical activity – swimming, dancing, riding a bike – that requires balance, timing and rhythm. Almost every mistake you can make in the golf swing – slicing, hooking, topping and that horror of horrors, shanking – can be traced back to a lack of balance, timing or rhythm.

What makes the golf swing such a maddeningly confusing thing to perfect is that not even championship golfers agree exactly on just how to go about it. Take the address. Three well-known Americans – Sam Snead, Ben Hogan and Jimmy Demaret – all went about it in a

41

different way. Snead aligned himself somewhat to the right of his target. Hogan was dead on line. Demaret aimed distinctly to the left of it. Needless to say, the ball usually ended up in the same place; which is to say, where the eyes were aiming.

Even on such an obviously important subject as timing there has always been wide disagreement. Neil Coles, one of Britain's most consistently successful players, has a full, measured swing; Peter Oosterhuis an abbreviated, flailing action; Christy O'Connor a smooth, rounded swing on the lazy side. Eddie Polland, one of the most improved players recently, a short, rapid punch.

Whatever any good player does physically during the golf swing, he always has only one thing uppermost in mind while he does it: hitting the ball. 'If I ever thought of anything else,' Bobby Jones once said, 'I didn't hit it.'

One of the great theorists of the game was the late Ernest Jones. The one imperative in golf, he argued, was to hit the ball. But if you swung the clubhead, the ball would take care of itself.

Jones lost a leg in World War I, and desperate to return to the game, off which he had made his living as a professional before the war, he forced himself to devise some method of hitting the ball while balanced on the leg he had left. Through trial and error he found out that he could keep his balance only when he concentrated hard on swinging the clubhead, dismissing everything else from his mind. Furthermore, when he concentrated only on swinging the clubhead, all the mechanics of the swing seemed to fall into their rightful place. In other words, the mechanics of a golf swing were not the cause of a good golf swing but the results of it. Swing the clubhead, he reasoned, and you can forget about everything else.

Jones taught his theory for nearly 50 years to golfers who were suffering, as he termed it, from 'paralysis by analysis'. They were ruining their golf swing by trying to divide it into the mechanical parts they thought made it up. 'You can't divide a golf swing into parts and still have a golf swing,' he said. 'Look! If you dissected a cat, you've got

Michelle Walker of Scotland – puttin

Figure 4. The golf swing—theory

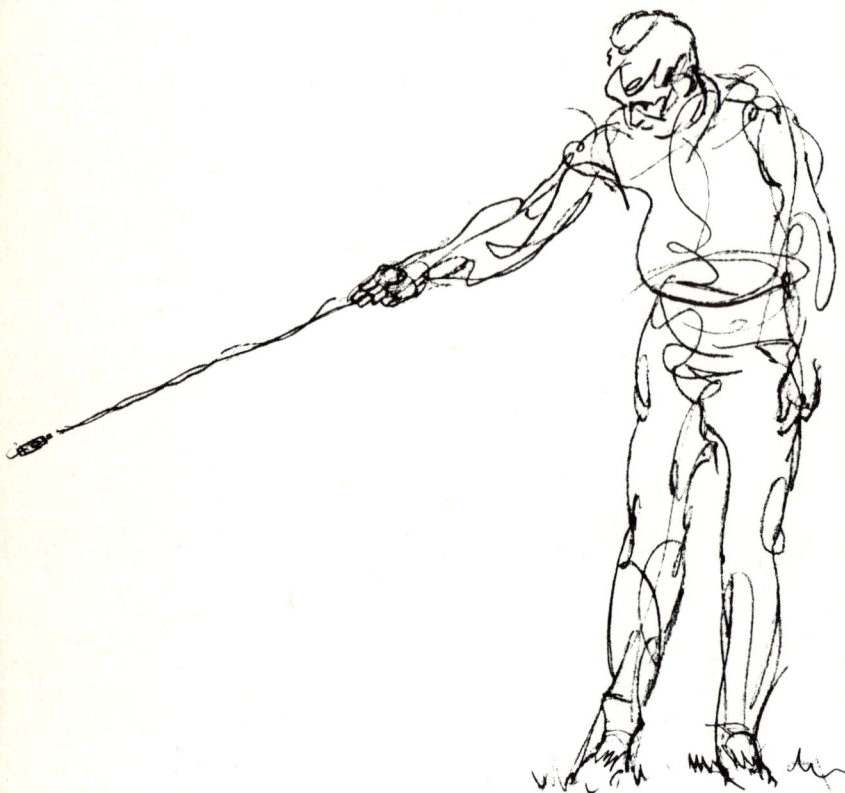

blood and guts and bones all over the place. But you haven't got a cat.'

To demonstrate what he considered to be the true swinging motion, Jones used to tie a penknife to the end of a handkerchief. Holding one end of the handkerchief between his thumb and his forefinger, he would swing the penknife back and forth, like a pendulum, Gradually lengthening the arc, he would point out that as long as he maintained the swinging motion the handkerchief would remain taut. Once, however, he attempted to add leverage – say, by jerking his hand – the handkerchief would collapse. Outside power, therefore, was not only super-fluous but undesirable. No matter how hard you try, you cannot move a penknife on the end of a handkerchief – or move a golf club – any faster than you can swing it. Why, then, try to do anything else? 'The golf swing is effortless power,' Jones said, 'not powerful effort.'

THE GRIP

The swing is begun by your hands. They have to begin it. After all, they are the only parts of your body attached to the club. The single most important fundamental in golf is the manner in which your hands are placed on the club – the grip. The grip determines your authority over the clubhead, which in turn determines the behaviour of the clubface, which determines the control of the ball.

Develop a sound grip, and all the other fundamentals of the swing fall into place. The nearest to a universal grip in golf is the 'Vardon' or overlapping grip. It derives its name from Harry Vardon, one of the great triumvirate who revolutionised golf form at the turn of the century. For seventy years it has proved to be the easiest way to hold on to the club as comfortably at the top of the backswing as at the beginning, without any loss of power or control at impact with the ball. Figure 6 shows how the little finger of your right hand should overlap the forefinger of your left, thus unifying your hands.

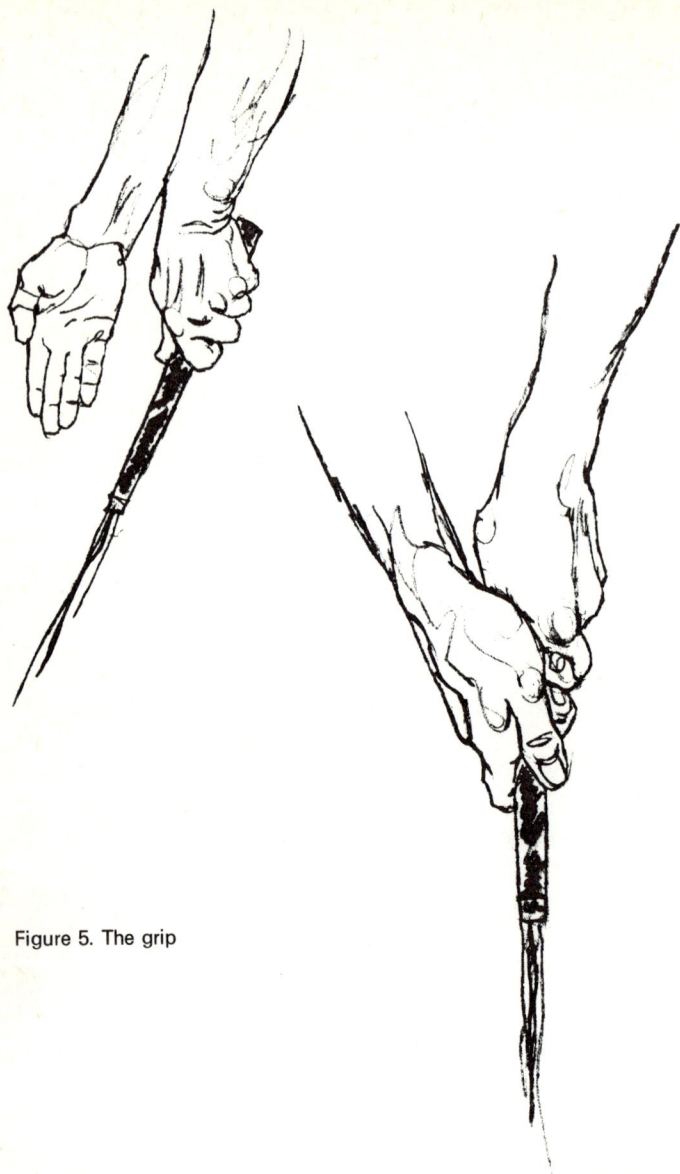

Figure 5. The grip

46

Figure 6. The overlapping, or so-called Vardon, grip

To the beginner, it seems an awkward way to hold anything, your natural tendency being to grab the club with your hands rather than grip it with your fingers. You need only hold the club in the palms of your hands – as you would a cricket bat – to realise how little control you have of the clubface. Squeeze it till your hands turn white, and a child can still twist the clubface at will.

No, what is needed is control through the fingers without any sacrifice in the natural power of the hands. The Vardon grip is the most effortless way to go about it.

Any grip, whether the Vardon or not, requires the back of your left hand and the front of your right hand to be aimed towards the target and the palms of both to be opposite one another (see Figure 7). In the Vardon grip your right, or lower, hand overlaps your left, but only in the sense that one finger overlaps it – the little finger of your right overlaps the forefinger of your left.

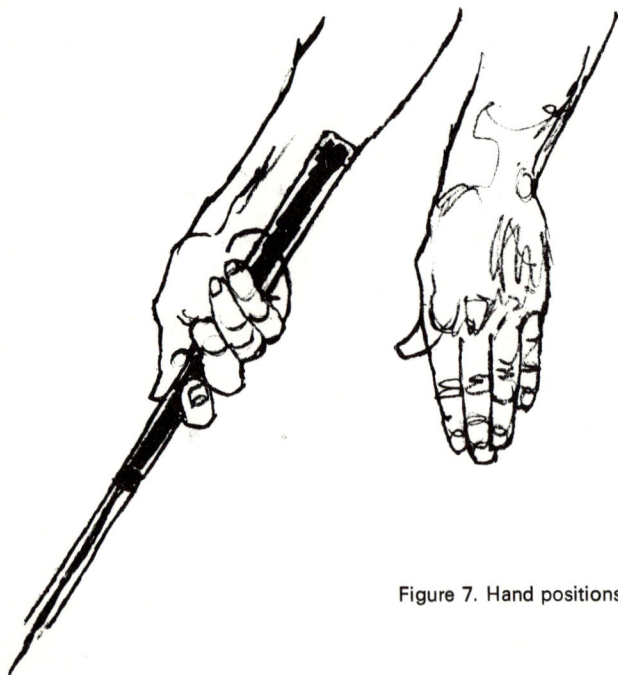

Figure 7. Hand positions

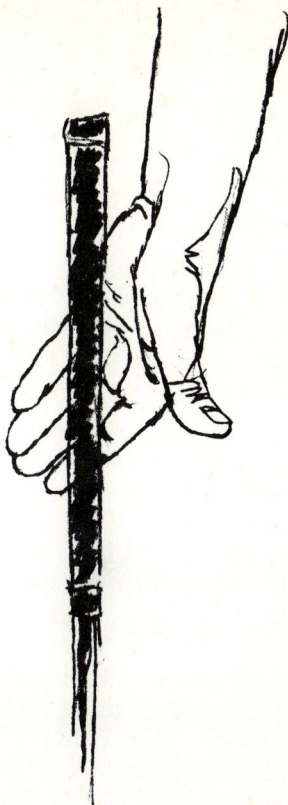

Figure 8. Assuming the grip

This overlapping accomplishes two objectives:
1 It helps to unify your hands, for golf is a two-handed game, with control derived mainly from your left and power mainly from your right, although each hand shares a measure of the other's responsibility.
2 It permits only four fingers of your right actually to be on the club at once, thereby diminishing the usually stronger right hand's tendency to overpower the usually weaker left.

As shown in Figure 8, the club is placed across the fingers of your left hand in such a manner that the pad of

49

your hand sits on top of it. Done properly, the club may be held at arm's length simply by crooking your forefinger underneath it without any help whatever from your remaining fingers. Your thumb is then clamped to the top of the shaft and placed in such a way that a distinct groove is formed between it and the back of your hand. When the clubhead is laid on the ground, this groove should point slightly right of your head – between it and your right shoulder.

Your right hand is placed on the club much in the manner of shaking hands. As pointed out, your little finger overlaps your left forefinger, riding in the groove formed by it and your left middle finger. The club is then squeezed by your fourth finger and the middle finger of your right hand, these two fingers being the chief sources through which the power of the right hand is transmitted. Your thumb and forefinger are then wrapped around the club until their tips touch, their primary role being to keep the clubface in its proper position as it is swung through the backswing and then whipped through the ball.

It is only through such a grip that you can, with any effective consistency, swing the clubhead, whether for a 'chip' of 30 feet, a 'pitch' of 30 yards or a 'drive' of 300 yards. No grip other than the Vardon, or a close approximation to it, allows for such a diversity among so many different types of people, regardless of height, weight, strength or hand size.

If your hands are the only parts of your body attached to the club, it must be kept in mind also that your feet are the only parts of your body attached to the ground. They have their job to do, too. One certain way to keep them from doing it properly is to place them haphazardly as you step up to the ball.

THE STANCE

A convenient method of learning how to place your feet correctly is to check yourself on the linoleum or other

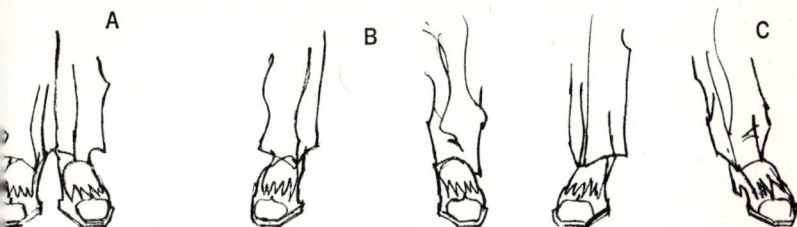

Figure 9. Feet positions

composition tiles usually found on bathroom or kitchen floors. Any flooring will do, so long as it has parallel lines.

Holding your feet together as though at attention (9A), spread them evenly apart until each comes to rest on a line about the width of your shoulders apart (B). Your feet now run squarely along the lines, neither flared out nor pigeon-toed. Then, leaving the right as it is, turn the toes of your left roughly 20 degrees to the left, in the direction in which you want the ball to go (C). With the weight of your body evenly distributed on both feet, as much on the heels as on the balls of them, this is the basic stance for every shot in golf.

There are various ramifications of this stance, notably for putting, chipping and pitching. But these are mere sophistications of the basic stance, each designed to make the player more comfortable as less of his body is called into use. (In putting, for example, you do not use your body at all.) If need be, you could play any of these side shots from the basic stance. But you could not play a full shot from any of its ramifications.

Flaring your left foot out serves its purpose, and so does keeping your right foot straight. As the club is swung back, a firm support is needed to balance the

51

Figure 10. Incorrect stance

Figure 11. Correct stance

Sandy Lyle – one of England's best young amateurs

weight of your body as the momentum of the clubhead forces it to pivot on your right knee, through the twisting of your hips and the simultaneous turning of your shoulders. This momentum also requires that your left knee tuck in so that it is pointing behind the ball, not stuck out so that it points in front of the ball. Tucked in in such a way, your left knee assists your right leg in supporting the weight of your body as the clubhead reaches the top of the backswing. Stuck straight out, it throws the preponderance of weight onto your left leg rather than 'behind' the ball, resulting in a multitude of sins, foremost among which is the probability that you will miss the ball entirely – an error that counts as a stroke just as much as a shot you knock into the hole. In golf, a 'stroke' is any motion made at the ball with the intent to hit it, regardless of the outcome. The drawings on pages 52 and 53 illustrate how your stance affects your swing.

THE ADDRESS

Having placed your feet properly on the ground, squarely along the desired line of flight, it becomes necessary to see that both your hips and shoulders are also aligned squarely with the line of flight. There should be nothing difficult about this procedure, for, once your feet are square, you need only stand straight to have your hips and shoulders square also (see Figure 12). However, since the shot is intended to go at right angles to the left, many golfers have a tendency to turn either their hips or their shoulders, or both, towards the target.

This is a particularly vicious habit among chronic slicers – those who show a marked tendency to hit the ball with left-to-right spin on it. They do this because, having flared the hips and shoulders out of alignment, they throw the clubhead outside the line of flight, causing it to cross the ball from outside the line to inside it, thereby causing it to spin and swerve from left to right (see Figure 13).

Figure 12. Correct alignment of feet, hips and shoulders

Figure 13. Incorrect alignment

It is easily the most common fault in golf. Ninety-nine out of every hundred golfers err in this direction. The other one per cent have to fight a natural tendency to hook the ball; that is, hit it with right-to-left spin. It is a phenomenon of golf, though, that from this small minority come practically all the good players in golf. The hook, then, is the bane of the expert. It is the slice you will have to worry about.

One handy way to check the alignment of your feet, hips and shoulders is simply to stand in a doorway as though you were about to address a ball, your body aligned with the sides of the doorway. Holding the club, you now reach for the ball by flexing your knees, as though you were about to dive off the side of a swimming pool. Turning your head from right to left, you can inspect your hips and shoulders to see if you have any tendency to flare them towards the target. This is the posture you must assume on the golf course, adjusting your sight to the target from it. Simply because you can see the target is no guarantee of the shot's success. After all, there are blind golfers who bring off perfect golf shots. They do so because they have aligned their bodies properly.

Flexing the knees is essential. It is the only method whereby you should reach for the ball as it lies on the ground. It should be done as though you were about to sit down but had changed your mind in the middle of doing so (see Figure 14), There is no bending over at your hips. Your back remains straight. The weight remains evenly distributed between the heels and the balls of your feet (see Figure 15). There is no sense of squatting or crouching. Rather, there is a sense of unreleased energy in your legs. You should feel as though your knees, hips and shoulders may be turned at will in either direction. Should someone ask you a question when you are in such a position, you should not feel as though you had to stand up to answer.

Once the clubhead is laid on the ground from this position, there should be no reaching for the ball. The

Figure 14. Incorrect stance—your knees should *not* be kept rigid

Figure 15. Incorrect stance—there should be no 'reaching' for the ball

clubhead should fall directly behind the ball without any other effort. If it does not, your entire body – not just one part of it – should be shifted until the clubface is where it should be. How far the ball should be from you is determined by your left arm, which is extended without becoming rigid. Once the swing has been set in motion, it is your left arm that will determine the radius of it, allowing the clubface to return squarely back to the ball.

Since your right hand will be lower on the club than your left, it should be placed on the club by lowering your right shoulder. It should not be placed on the club by jutting your right shoulder out towards the ball. This action throws your shoulders entirely out of position. In point of fact, it puts them into the dreaded slice position.

One sure indication as to whether or not your stance is correct is the position of your hands at the address; or, more particularly, the position of your wrists. They should be set in such a way that the club seems to become a straight extension of your arms. If there are wrinkles, this means your wrists are bent, thereby breaking the radius of the swing you want to establish with your left arm. In short, you are crouching.

Every shot in golf should be addressed in an attitude of calm expectancy. Your body should be relaxed but not loose, firm but not taut. For, in essence, a golf swing consists of two motions: a backswing and a downswing. In the former, tension is built up. In the latter, it is released. In the former, energy is stored up by your muscles. In the latter, it is transmitted by the muscles of your body through your hands to the shaft out of the clubhead into the ball.

Many beginners, and not a few veteran players who never seem to improve, spoil this energy-building process by becoming too tense before the swing has begun. They grip the club tight in an effort to make it feel lighter than it is. Consequently, they fail to generate any tension during the backswing and so have no energy to deliver to the ball in the downswing.

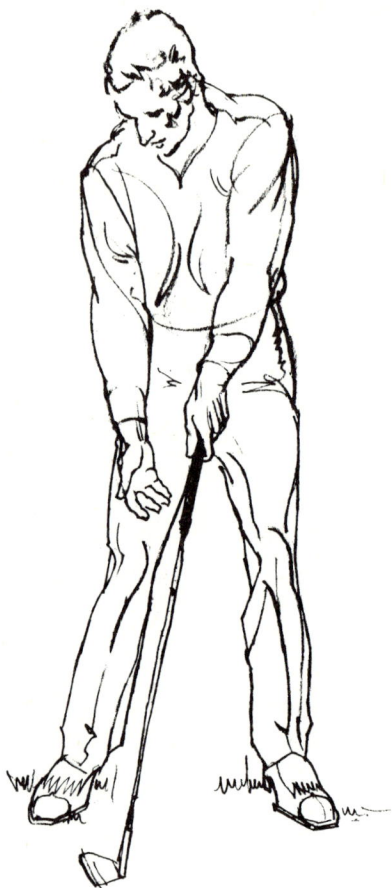

Figure 16. Correct stance—place your right hand on the club by lowering your right shoulder

Figure 17. Incorrect stance—do *not* place your right hand on the club by jutting your right shoulder out

A golf club should never be gripped any tighter than the grip used to shake hands with a lady. After all, a golf club weighs less than a pound, or less than a tennis racquet. Because most of its weight is concentrated in the head, however, it should feel heavier than it actually is. It is this feel of the clubhead that permits you to generate clubhead speed, that permits you to swing the club rather than merely hit with it. Remember, it is physically impossible to move the clubhead any faster than you can swing it – which helps explain why golf is almost unique among sports in that a good little man is at little or no disadvantage to a good big man. On anybody's list of the ten greatest players in the history of the game, it is unlikely that more than one of them would stand more than 5 feet 11 or weigh more than 190 pounds.

THE WAGGLE

Unnecessary tension in the address can be dispersed through what is known as the 'waggle' (see Figure 18). This is a preliminary motion – a kind of swing in miniature – during which you imitate the path you want the clubhead to follow during the first 2 feet of the backswing.

It is performed entirely by the hands and wrists. The wrists are cocked backwards and forwards, but not up and down, as the clubhead describes the first 20 degrees or so of the arc you want it to take when you initiate your backswing.

In addition to relieving tension, the waggle helps to establish the tempo you want to maintain throughout the entire swing.

Additionally, it serves as a double check on your distance from the ball. As the clubhead is waggled back and forth, the centre of the clubface – the 'sweet spot' – should return precisely to the belly of the ball. The sweet spot is where the weight of the clubhead is concentrated and, hence, is where the preponderance of the club's mechanical energy is stored.

Figure 18. The 'waggle' stance

Figure 19. The 'waggle' action

THE BACKSWING

The backswing evolves out of the motion established by the waggle. This is to say, you should go directly into the backswing from a series of waggles without pausing. Keep uppermost in mind that the backswing is just that: a swing. It is not a lifting action or any other type of action. It is a swing pure and simple, something that cannot be seen or photographed or described in words. You can only feel it.

There are two points to bear in mind which are of great assistance in making sure the golf swing is a swing throughout its entirety. They are a sure grip on the club and a stationary head position. You should be distinctly conscious of your hands on the club throughout the entire swing, even when they are behind your head. And your head should feel as though it were suspended in space.

This feeling is particularly crucial at the start of the downswing, which is a stage when many golfers have a tendency to duck their heads in an often disastrous effort to elevate the ball. All the loft necessary for any golf shot has been built into the clubface. All you can do is move the ball forwards. While your head may move back and forth to a degree, it must not be permitted to move up or down. Moving it up causes you to top the ball, moving it down causes you to hit behind the ball, among other things. If your head is held relatively stationary, you should be able to see plainly the dimples on the ball throughout the entire swing.

While the backswing is initiated by your hands – and followed in turn by your arms, shoulders and hips in natural anatomical order – it is accomplished by all these factors working in unison. Ideally, your shoulders should turn twice as far as your hips. Theoretically, although this is not always physically possible, your shoulders should turn a full 90 degrees, while your hips should turn 45 degrees. This position places your hands

Figure 20. The backswing action

Figure 21. In the backswing, your muscles, stretching from a relaxed position, store up energy

just behind your right ear, your left shoulder just under your chin. The weight of your body should now be braced by your right leg, which is still in the flexed position it was at the address, and is supported by the inside of your left foot, particularly by the joint of your big toe.

At the top of the backswing, a distinct feeling of unreleased tension should be felt in your shoulders, particularly along your left shoulder and through your left arm. Somewhat less tension should be felt in your hips, but it should be distinct nonetheless, particularly in your left hip. It is the unleashing of this tension that will initiate the downswing, in a manner that is almost entirely instinctive.

THE DOWNSWING

The downswing, of course, is the backswing in reverse anatomical order. Therefore, it is initiated by your hips. While your hands are held stationary somewhere behind your right ear, your left hip is twisted back towards the target so that your left heel returns precisely to the position it was at the address. As your hips pass a line parallel to the intended line of flight, your shoulders, in natural order, begin to turn towards the target also. They, in their turn, pull your arms and hands down parallel to the ground. All this has been accomplished without any conscious throwing of your hands or arms towards the ball. The feeling is almost as though the club had purposely been left at the top of the backswing. You cannot actually do this, of course, but that is nevertheless the feeling. It is the trunk of your body that has done all the work, instinctively unleashing all the tension that has been built into it by the backswing. You have arrived at the moment of truth in the golf swing.

The weight of your body has been returned almost completely to your left side. It is braced by your left leg, which is still in the flexed position it was at the address, and is supported by your right foot, particularly by the joint of your big toe – just the reverse of the position on

Figure 22. The downswing, in which your muscles transmit energy through your hands to the shaft, out of the clubhead into the ball

the backswing. Your right knee has been tucked in towards your left knee and is already well past the ball.
Your head is still stationary. Your hands are at hip
level. The shaft of the club is parallel to the ground.

At this stage, you have generated so much motion –
swinging motion – that only a conscious effort can disturb
the clubhead from striking the ball in the manner you
had acted out with the preliminary waggle. You need only
swing *through* the ball. There is no necessity to swing
at it.

There is a long list of 'Don'ts' associated with arriving
at the moment of truth in the downswing. Chief among
them would be:

1 Don't try to throw the clubhead at the ball with your
  hands from the top of the backswing. If you do this,
  you succeed only in throwing it outside the line of
  flight, resulting in either a slice or a darting hook, the
  former caused by an open clubface and the latter by a
  shut clubface. Furthermore, you dissipate a great deal
  of clubhead speed.
2 Don't try to help the ball into the air.
  Both these errors – and a lot of others – can be eliminated by two positive movements:

1 Leave the clubhead at the top of the backswing until
  the weight of your body has been shifted to your left
  side, spinning your left hip out of the way. By leaving
  the clubhead behind you, so to speak, until the preponderance of your weight has shifted to your left
  side, the clubhead remains inside the intended line
  of flight until impact.
2 Consciously tuck your right knee towards your left
  knee well in advance of hitting the ball. By tucking
  your right knee towards your left before you make
  impact, you have eliminated any tendency to keep
  your weight on your right side, which is the only
  position from which you can, consciously or un-
  consciously, scoop the ball into the air. Even if, by

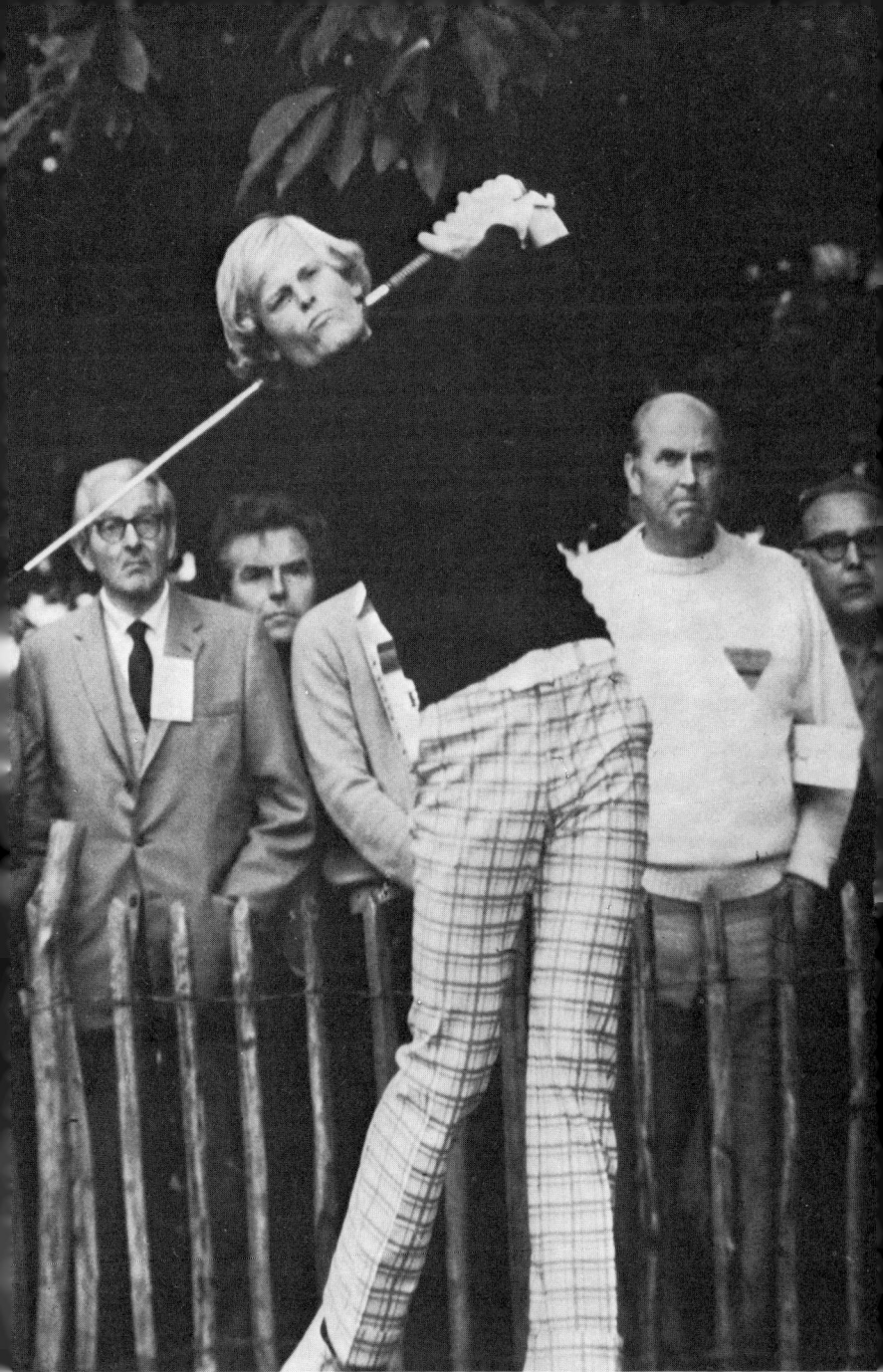

Johnny Miller — a full follow-through

Figure 23. The finish of the follow-through

accident, you make solid contact with the ball by scooping it, at best you have only succeeded in turning a five iron, say, into a six iron. And what is the point in that?

THE FOLLOW-THROUGH

The finish of the golf swing – the 'follow-through' – obviously contributes nothing towards hitting the ball, since the ball is well on its way by the time you arrive at the follow-through. But the correct follow-through serves its purpose nevertheless.

All truly polished players are conspicuous for the gracefulness of their follow-through. Their weight is perfectly balanced on their left leg, they are standing in an upright position, their hands are high above their head, right arm extended, the left tucked into their side (see Figure 23). They have been able to arrive at this position because everything that preceded it was executed correctly. If they do not arrive at this position, they check backwards to try to find out what went wrong.

Let us assume, for instance, that the bulk of your weight still remains on your right leg instead of your left. This result would be impossible had you tucked your right knee towards your left before you hit the ball.

Or let us assume that your hands have finished low – say, somewhere in the vicinity of your left shoulder. They could not have finished in this position if the clubhead had been left at the top of the swing when you initiated the downswing with your left hip.

And on it goes. The correct follow-through is the result of a correct downswing. If it is incorrect, check backwards to find out why.

PITCH SHOTS AND CHIP SHOTS

Pitch shots and chip shots are golf shots in capsule form. Since they are played from distances of a hundred yards down to only a few feet, their primary purpose is accuracy.

Figure 24. The chip shot

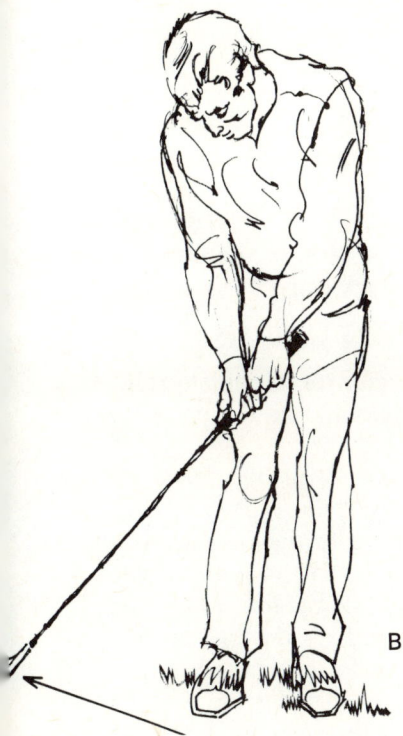

B

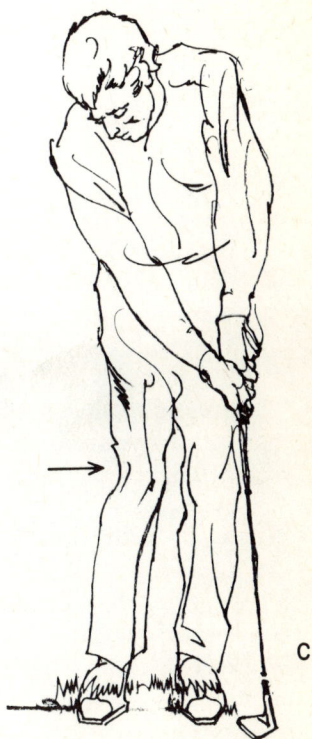

C

Consequently, a pitch is played with a backswing only three-quarters or half as long as normal, depending upon the distance required for the shot. Although the standard address is used, your feet are much closer together in the stance, since little or no shifting of weight to your right side will be required on the backswing.

There must nevertheless be a distinct sensation of moving to your left side on the downswing. The clubhead must feel as though it were being left behind as your left hip moves past the ball. And your right knee should tuck in towards your left before contact is made with the ball.

All this is as it would be with any golf shot. Golfers who fail to execute these two movements have a tendency to 'wheel' on the ball with a pitch; which is to say, they lock their hips and throw the clubhead outside the line of flight. The result is that they often hit the ball in a sort of roundhouse action or hit it cleanly without benefit of backspin.

The pitch is more often than not played with the pitching wedge, the most lofted club in the bag. People who never seem to get the knack of pitching are people who never put complete faith in this loft. They invariably try to hit the ball higher than the clubface will permit it to go, and, as a result, lose control of the shot. Think only of hitting the ball forwards and let the clubface get it into the air for you.

The chip shot is a miniature form of the pitch. Its purpose is to loft the ball over a few feet of fairway or rough until the ball bounces on to the putting surface, thereafter running to the hole just like a putt. It should be played with practically no body action at all. Figure 24A shows how you should address the ball with your feet together, your hands well down the shaft. The backswing is slight, accomplished solely by your hands and arms (B). The shot is struck crisply, again with little or no body movement, although your right knee should be allowed to tuck into your left as you swing through the ball (C).

Lee Trevino – playing a pitch and run shot

Although pitches and chips are played purely for accuracy's sake, they must nevertheless be executed with authority. They should be hit briskly, with your arms and hands, although no power is needed. If they are not, the ball will be struck sloppily without backspin and will not have the braking power to stop on a putting surface.

PUTTING

Putting is the most highly instinctive form of golf there is. Very few people can teach someone else to putt. Putting

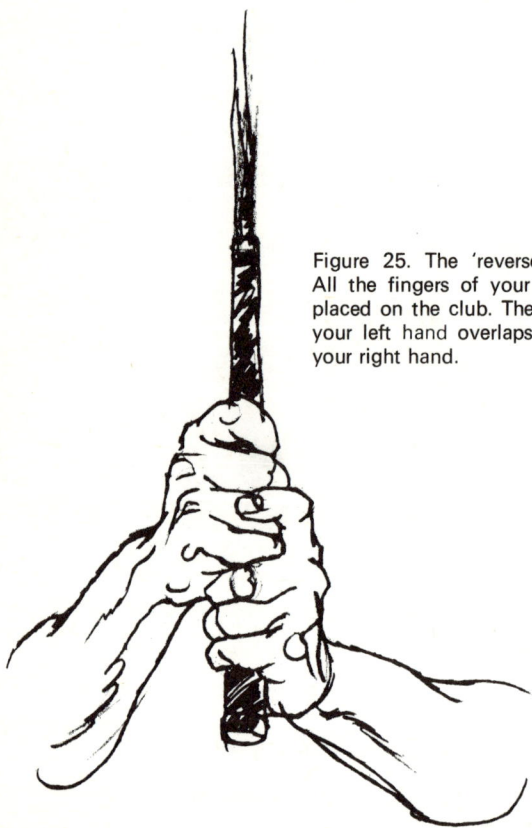

Figure 25. The 'reverse overlap' grip. All the fingers of your right hand are placed on the club. The index finger of your left hand overlaps two fingers of your right hand.

is largely a matter of developing a comfortable style, and may be as individualistic as your handwriting.

Successful putting depends upon a consistent method and an ability to 'read the green' – to judge the correct path along which the ball should be hit if it is to drop into the hole.

The putting stroke should be smooth and rhythmic, and the ball struck solidly with the centre of gravity (the sweet spot) of the club, the blade of which must be square

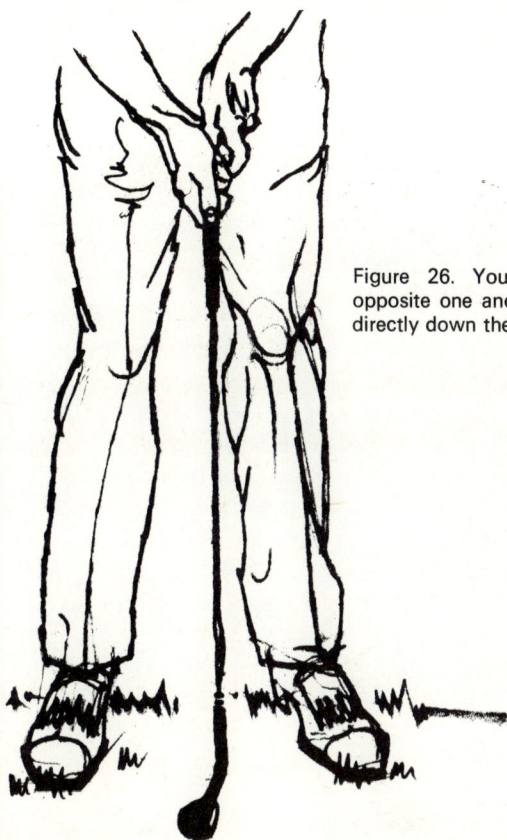

Figure 26. Your hands are directly opposite one another; thumbs pointing directly down the shaft

81

to the intended direction of the ball at impact. Some excellent players like to give the ball a sharp tap, others prefer a longer stroke. Several use their wrists in effecting the stroke, while others keep their wrists locked firmly, except on extremely long putts. Select whichever method is best for you, but be sure that you are consistent.

While most golfers err in their shots by trying to hit the ball into the air, they usually err in their putts by trying to hit the ball into the green, rather than along its surface. This is best accomplished by forcing yourself, regardless of how you putt, to keep the clubhead as close to the ground as possible throughout the entire stroke.

One help in doing this is to alter your grip until your palms are opposite each other with your thumbs pointed straight down the shaft. With their hands in this position, many top players further alter their grips by reversing the overlap. This is to say, they overlap one or two fingers of their right hand with their left index finger, rather than have the little finger of their right hand overlap the left.

Very few putts will run for more than a few feet in an absolutely straight line. Almost all greens have undulations, an overall slope, or even the problem of 'grain'. Grain – the direction in which the blades of grass of the green are growing – imparts bias to the roll of the ball. The harder the putt is hit, the less it will deviate from its path – but the further it will go if it misses the hole. Reading the green is a skill which can be developed with practice, but it is usually worth looking at a putt from both sides of the hole and considering any special features which may exist, such as the proximity of the sea, or the overall lie of the land, if in any doubt. Greens nearly always slope towards the sea and away from the side of the hill into which they have been cut.

So that is the game of golf – perverse, infuriating and wholly satisfying. It now remains only to play it.

Gary Player – lining up a putt

Jack Nicklaus in pensive mood

4   Useful Information

ASSOCIATIONS

The Royal and Ancient Golf Club
Sec: K R T Mackenzie MC
    St Andrews
    Fife

Governing body of the game and the authority on Rules of Golf and Rules of Amateur Status.

The English Golf Union
Sec: Ian Erskine
    12a Denmark Street
    Wokingham
    Berkshire RG11 2BE

The Welsh Golfing Union
Sec: J. W. Trehane
    2 Isfrym
    Bury Port
    Carmarthenshire

The Scottish Golf Union
Sec: J Forman
    23 Newington Road
    Edinburgh EH9 1QR

The Golfing Union of
Ireland
Sec: W A Menton
    Glencar House
    81 Eglington Road
    Dublin 4

The National Golf Unions, which are concerned with the general administration of the amateur game within each country of the British Isles.

The Ladies Golf Union
Sec: Miss K Hannay
    2 Fairways

Sandwich Bay
Kent

Concerned with administration of the game, so far as ladies are concerned, both at home and abroad.

The Professional Golfers' Association
Sec: C Snape BCom
          National Headquarters
          The Kennington Oval
          Kennington
          London SE11 5ST

Official association for professional golfers in the country.

The Golf Development Council
Sec: G A McPartlin OBE
          London Scottish Golf Club
          Windmill Enclosure
          Wimbledon Common
          London SW19 5NQ

Represents all major governing bodies of the sport. Amongst other services it gives technical advice to local authorities and to clubs on the siting and establishment of golf courses. Also administers the Coaching Award for teachers in schools.

The Golf Foundation
Sec: G A McPartlin OBE
          Allington House
          136–142 Victoria Street
          London SW1E 5LD

Encourages competitive golf in schools and assists in the formation of county schools' Golf Association. Subsidises professional instruction, given by members of the PGA.

BOOK LIST

Reference and Technical

The Golfers' Handbook. Lists names and addresses of all golf clubs in the United Kingdom, as well as Golfing Unions, Associations and other organisations, etc.
Golf Rules Illustrated (Munro-Barr Publications Ltd). The official publication of the Royal & Ancient Golf Club.
Technical pamphlets available through the Golf Development Council:
a *Elements of Golf Course Layout and Design*
b *Golf Clubhouses – A Planning Guide*
c *Guide to Group Coaching*
d *Golf Teaching Kit*
e *Golf Instructor's Guide*
f *Visual Aids for Golf Instruction*

Instructional

How to Play Your Best Golf all the Time by Tommy Armour (Hodder & Stoughton) (Coronet).
Golf My Way by Jack Nicklaus.
Practical Golf by John Jacobs (Stanley Paul).

Courses

The Golf Course Guide by Donald Steel (Collins/Daily Telegraph).
Play the Best Courses by Peter Allen (Stanley Paul).
Frank Pennink's Choice of Golf Courses by Frank Pennink (A & C Black).

Magazines

Golf Illustrated published weekly.
Golf International published weekly.
Golf Monthly published monthly.
Golf World published monthly.

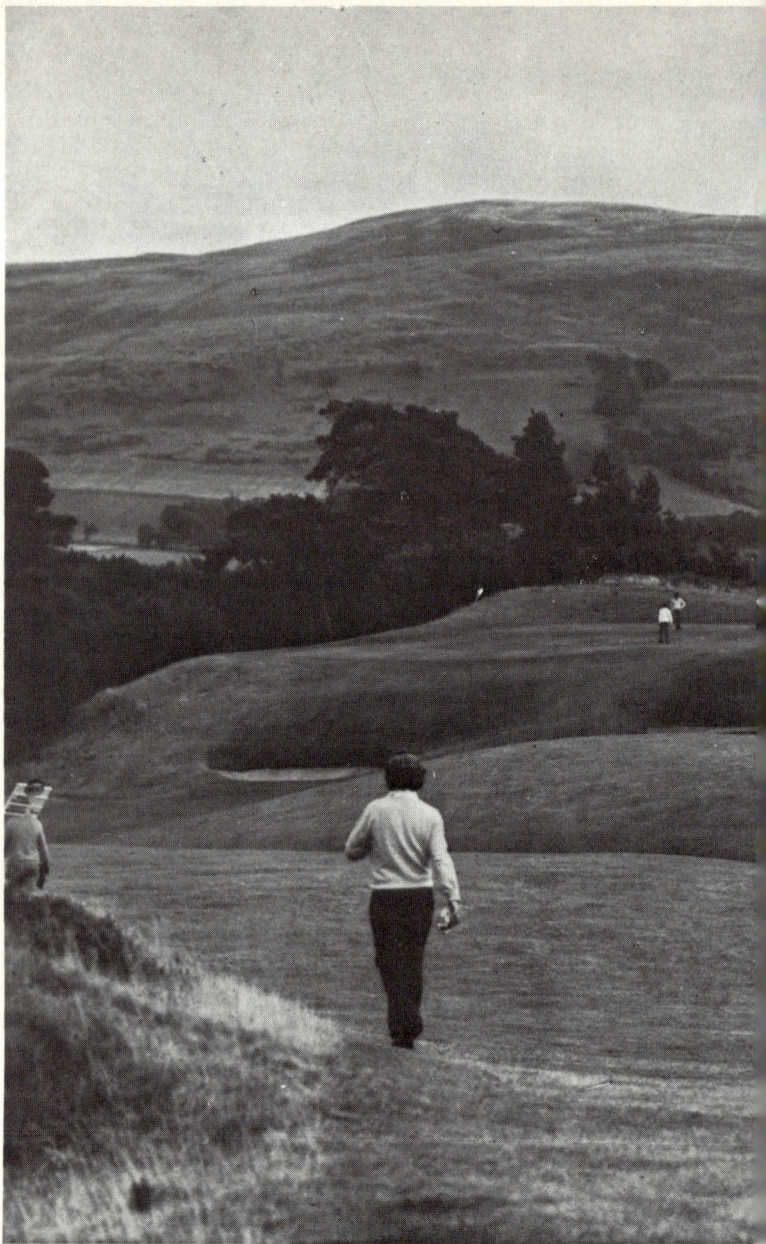

The King's Course at Gleneagles

Catherine Lacoste of France

Glossary of Golf Terms

ACE. Slang for a hole-in-one.

ADDRESS. The position in which a player puts himself in order to strike the ball.

ALBATROSS. A hole played in three strokes less than par.

APPROACH. A shot, usually quite short, aimed at the green.

AWAY. A player whose ball lies farthest from the hole is said to be away.

BEST-BALL MATCH. One in which one player competes against the better ball of two – or three – other players.

BIRDIE. A hole played in one stroke less than par.

BLIND. A term describing a hole or shot when its green or finish cannot be seen by the player striking the ball.

BOGEY. One over par.

BUNKER. An area of ground usually covered with sand.

CADDIE. A person who carries the player's clubs.

CARRY. The distance from where a ball is hit to where it first strikes the ground.

CHIP. A short approach shot where the ball is made to bounce and then roll along the ground.

COURSE. The terrain over which play is permitted.

CROSS-BUNKER. A narrow bunker that crosses a hole at a right angle to the player's line of fire to the putting surface.

CUPPY. A lie in which the ball sits in a small depression in the ground.

DEAD. A ball so near the hole that the holing of the putt is considered a certainty.

DIVOT. A piece of turf sliced off while playing a stroke.

DOG LEG. A hole whose fairway is marked by a bend.

DRAW. A slight hook in the flight of a ball.

EAGLE. A hole played in two strokes less than par on a par-four or par-five.

FACE. The surface of the head of the club with which the ball is struck.

FAIRWAY. The expanse of ground between the teeing ground and the putting green, which is especially prepared for play.

FLAGSTICK. A movable indicator centred in the hole to show its position on the green.

FOLLOW-THROUGH. The continuation of the swing after the ball has been struck.

FORE! A cry of warning to other players or to spectators.

FOUR-BALL MATCH. One in which two play their better ball against the better ball of two other players.

FOURSOME. A match in which two play against two, each side playing one ball with alternate strokes.

GREEN. The surface specially prepared for putting.

GRIP. The part of the shaft that is held in the hands. Also the grasp itself.

HALF-SHOT. A shot played with less than a full swing.

HALVE. A hole is said to be halved if each side holes out in the same number of strokes.

HANDICAP. The number of strokes over par in which one's average game is played. This number may be deducted from a player's actual score in a stroke play completion.

HANGING. A lie in which a ball is situated on a slope inclining downwards.

HAZARD. An area, such as a bunker or a pond, in which the privileges of play are restricted.

HEAD. The part of the club which strikes the ball.

HEEL. The part of the face of a club nearest the shaft.

HOLE. In general, the part of the course from the tee to the putting surface. Also the circular opening, or cup, in the green into which the ball is played. It is $4\frac{1}{4}$ inches in diameter.

HOLE-IN-ONE. A hole on which the tee shot goes into the hole.

HOLE OUT. To make the stroke that puts the ball into the cup.

HONOUR. The privilege of playing first from a tee, which cannot be declined.

HOOK. To hit the ball with a right-to-left spin, so that it curves to the left of the line of flight.

HOSEL. The socket into which the shaft of an iron is fitted.

IN. A term referring to the second nine holes of a golf course, as opposed to the first nine.

IRONS. Clubs with metal blades for heads.

LIE. The state of the ball's position on the ground.

LINE. The direction in which the player intends the ball to travel after it is hit.

LINKS. Originally, a course laid out on linksland, the sandy soil deposited by centuries of receding tides. Today a synonym for any golf course.

LOFT. Any angle less than 90 degrees on the face of a club. Also, to hit the ball with a high trajectory.

MARKER. A scorer in stroke play who is appointed by the tournament committee to record a competitor's score. He may be a fellow-competitor. He is *not* a referee or a forecaddie.

MATCH. A contest between two players, or between a player and a side, or between two sides, which is determined by the number of holes won and lost.

MATCH PLAY. A tournament or championship conducted under the rules of match rather than those of stroke play.

NASSAU. Three matches in one. One point is allotted for the first nine holes, another point for the second nine, and still another for the over-all eighteen.

ODD, THE. A stroke more than the opponent played.

OUT. A term referring to the first nine holes of a golf course, as opposed to the second nine.

PAR. The number of strokes an expert golfer is expected to make on each hole. It is determined primarily by the length of the hole.

Tom Weiskopf helping Jack Nicklaus line up a putt during the Ryder Cup

94

PITCH. An approach shot where the ball is lofted into the air.

PITCH-AND-RUN. A shot so played that the ball covers part of the desired distance in the air and part by rolling along the ground.

PITCHING WEDGE. The iron with the most loft, used for short, high shots.

POT BUNKER. A small, deep sand trap.

PULL. A wide, pronounced hook.

PUSH. A shot that travels on a straight line but well to the right of the intended line.

PUTT. Any short stroke in which the ball rolls along the ground. Usually confined to specially prepared greens.

PUTTER. A straight-faced club, or one with very little loft, with which the ball is putted.

ROUGH. The part of the course that is not tee, fairway, green or hazard.

RUB OF THE GREEN. Any chance deflection of the ball while it is in play.

RUN. The distance the ball rolls after striking the ground.

RUN-UP. An approach in which the ball travels close to or on the ground.

SAND WEDGE. An iron that is used to extricate the ball from sand, or heavy rough.

SCRATCH. A standard of play equal to par, for which no handicap strokes are granted.

SCRATCH PLAYER. A player whose handicap is zero.

SHAFT. The part of the club that is not the head.

SHANK. The part of the hosel nearest the face. Also, to hit the ball on the shank.

SHORT GAME. Pitching, chipping and putting.

SINGLE. A match between two players.

SLICE. To hit the ball in such a way that it has left-to-right spin, and swerves to the right of the line of flight.

SOCKET. The opening in the neck of an iron club into which the shaft is fitted. Sometimes also used in the same sense as shank.

SOLE. The bottom of the club.

STROKE. A forward movement of a club, made with the intention of hitting the ball. Whether successful or not, it counts.

STROKE PLAY. A competition in which the player's total score for the round is compared with the scores of other players in the field.

SWING. The movement of the club in the operation of hitting the ball.

TEE. The peg on which the ball is usually placed for the first shot to each hole.

TEEING GROUND. The starting place for the hole to be played.

THREE-BALL MATCH. One in which three players compete against each other, with each playing his own ball.

THREESOME. A match in which one player competes against two others on one side, the two playing alternate strokes with the same ball.

THROUGH THE GREEN. The whole course except for the tee, hazards and the green.

TOP. To hit the ball above its centre.

WHIPPING. The thread or twine used to wrap the area where the head and shaft of the club are joined together.